Keep Him Coming Home with Love

The Warmth of Your Home Determines
the Temperature of Your Relationship

Shenitha Finesse Anniece Burton

S.H.E. PUBLISHING, LLC

For more information, contact:
info@shepublishingllc.com
www.shepublishingllc.com

Cover design by Michelle Phillips of CHELLD3
3D VISUALIZATION AND DESIGN

Isbns:
Paperback (*She*Edition): 978-1-7350327-5-7
eBook: 978-1-7350327-6-4
Paperback 978-1-7350327-7-1

First Edition: November 2020
Revised Edition | 2022

This book is dedicated to a phenomenal woman, a woman who has shown me that the best things in life are free, one of which has been her unconditional love for me. My mother is a woman who shares the mysteries of her history, a human who is not perfect, and like all of us, she has made some imperfect decisions but continues to know her worth. To understand my mother's love is to see that she will always be a part of me, and when we no longer share this space on earth, her light will shine from within me and my offspring. I can see the beauty of my mother's fragile heart, and I only wish I could have wiped away her tears and hurts when she could only see the reflection of her mother's face within her dreams. Because of my mother, my queen, I am a stronger woman today and will forever thank *God* for our union. Everybody has a unique story to tell, and this story is about a little girl who has grown into an extraordinary woman because of another woman's sacrifice.

Table of Contents

Introduction

Salute! You have begun part II of *Keep Him Coming Home with Love*. Part I focused on being intentional about strengthening the bond between you and your significant other. Part II is about going beyond him or her, finding yourself, and focusing on the surroundings that feed your soul.

The connection of part I and part II is the beginning of a journey that's simultaneous. These two stories complement each other, and you can't have one without the other. There are moments within these shared stories that have proven to me that the warmth of your home determines the temperature of your relationship. I've learned that you must value the real estate of your home and your marriage by designating rooms of passion and peace, observing serenity, valuing relationships, and keeping your emotional bank account at a positive balance at all times.

Keep Him Coming Home with Love is a four-book series, and in this book, we will focus on *love*:

Living room décor;

Observing serenity;

Valuing Relationships; and

Evening tones with a splash of color.

As you begin to read this book, I charge you with being intentional about the new memories you create within each room of your home. Be reflective and transparent as you begin to think about how you and others may feel when they enter the doors of your palace and whether those feelings, thoughts, and emotions will *keep him coming home with love*.

Chapter One

The Journey of L:
Living Room Décor

Your home should tell the story of who you are and be a

collection of what you love brought together under one roof.

—Nate Berkus

I f the walls of your home could speak, what would they say? From the crevices of their corners, to the wallpaper or base paint, to the crown moldings or tray ceilings, what secrets would they share?

The room décor of your living spaces can affect the tone of your relationship. Over the years of my marriage, I began to compare the décor of our homes to the décor of our relationship.

It amazes me how a piece of furniture placed in an empty room can make the room look bigger or how the boldness of color on an accent wall can make a room look wide open, warm, and welcoming or cluttered, closed, and cold. Strategically placing furniture within the rooms of your living quarters, selecting distinct colors for your walls, creating a pleasant aroma within your home, and designating rooms of passion and peace can *contribute* to the success of your relationship.

Jermaine and I have shared three homes thus far, and as our relationship grew, so did our homes, each marking the beginning of a new phase in our life together. The first home we shared was an apartment within a three-story complex. Its structure was more than enough space for both of us and our firstborn, Jada. We were lucky to have access to a pool and grilling areas, as we loved to throw our baby girl big birthday parties every year. During that moment in my marriage, the importance of the décor of our home never once crossed my mind. If the walls of our apartment could speak, they would tell you of the fun moments we shared, my laughter from Jermaine's comical personality, and the meetings that we held planning our present and future together. On the other hand, the secrets from the crevices of its corners would share the moments of struggle, which included meetings with our pastor who counseled us within our storms and passionate conversations in front of our children that ultimately led to our separation in mind, body, and soul. Jermaine remains to be that fine light-skinned hunk of a man that I love, and yes, we are still married at this moment. Nevertheless, during those times of struggle, the spice and passion that led us to marriage changed into a place of bitterness and darkness, not unlike the black furniture that cluttered our apartment.

Home number two would be the "Burton Mansion," our townhome. This home's architecture included high vaulted ceilings, a skylight that spotlighted our long staircase, and a narrow hallway that led to our shared living areas. At that time, my conservative taste would lead me to decorate our home with historical furniture that complemented the dark chardonnay-colored accent wall. The way I decorated our home mimicked what I'd seen displayed on the television. Not to mention, every room in home number two bore the distraction of a television and was open grounds for those difficult conversations. If I could do it all over again, the décor of our home would tell our story and mirror the uniqueness of who we are.

When it came to home number three, our single-family home we called the "Lake House," I decided to be mindful of how I decorated my living room and the other rooms within our home. My goal was to create a space to fill with memories of fun and feelings of tranquility. I would also designate rooms of war and passion because those moments within any relationship are inevitable.

Home number three was a milestone moment in our lives. We renewed our vows, and we began to clearly communicate our expectations and the boundaries within each room of our home. This adjustment would lead to a sacred and pleasant domicile for myself and our children, and it would, without a doubt, *keep him coming home with love.*

Moment One:
The Entrance to the Kingdom

———— ⧆ ————

The warmth of your home determines the temperature

of your relationship.

—Shenitha Finesse Anniece Burton

Imagine the smell of a tender piece of steak cooking on the stovetop submerged under a fresh bed of green peppers and onions. Although that is the meal's main course, it does not take away from the delicious mashed potatoes and vegetable medley. As Jermaine entered the doors of our lake house, he looked forward to being greeted by his children and his wifey, *me*. He'd smell the aroma of dinner prepared, and he'd see the soft light that illuminated the entrance to our home, which created a tranquil ambiance that framed the feeling of warmth and love. It gave affirmation to him that *there is no place like home.*

With my demanding career working for the federal judiciary, having four daughters, and my businesses, this had become somewhat of a struggle to manage. So there were times when he cooked or we ate out, but on those days when I successfully created a serene ambiance, I pulled out all the stops. And when I did, I needed to be a sight for sore eyes after his long day at work.

The entrance to our kingdom was picture-perfect. Our living room décor included a white leather sectional that I'd separated to form two furniture pieces. The sectional was set parallel and facing each other for those light-hearted conversations. I'd also added the warmth of a fireplace made of white wood and brick material, a tall standing plant that added a touch of nature, and a midsize burnt orange vase that unveiled a splash of color. I placed canvas art of our family photos on the wall, and the unique piece of furniture that would tell our story would be a piano, which represents how great of a team we are when we are in perfect harmony. *I am the treble, and he is the bass.*

We were finally beginning to value the real estate of our home and our marriage, and it was perfect timing for what was about to happen next. I met Nene Morris, the author of *My Marriage Planner*. *My Marriage Planner* is a journal that gives you innovative ideas on how to explore the journey of marriage together. The concept of this journal is to encourage you to take the time and make an effort to plan your marriage, just as you did to plan your wedding. This journal provided me with the strategies I knew I had not embarked on within my marriage. *My Marriage Planner* became a reminder to me that journaling is a profound way to reflect on your relationship and can be used as a tool for self-counseling. This newfound knowledge helped me continue to be mindful of the details of my marriage, which also included the décor of our home.

Moment Two:
Rooms of Passion and Peace

❦

Be selective with your battles. Sometimes peace is

better than being right.

—Unknown

The moment I walked into our lake house, I knew it was a place where we belonged. I could feel the positive energy bouncing off the walls. I didn't want to make the same mistake in this house that I'd made in our first two homes, where we selfishly continued to display undesirable behavior and tainted every room in our home with uncontrollable emotions of negativity. So in this home, I finally decided to designate rooms of passion and rooms of peace.

Establishing a set place to accomplish specific tasks is a great benefit, I'd say. Just as the kitchen is a place to cook and eat, and the bathroom is a place to bathe, I designated rooms for prayer, fun, family meetings, education, and, most importantly, the rooms for war, *disagreements*. My grandmother Mabel used to say, "there is a time and a place for everything."

The beauty of a new day is that you have another

opportunity to make it right, with the hopes that too much damage was not done yesterday. So if I'd tainted a room I considered to be special and sacred, I would press the reset button and start again. I'd do this by rearranging the furniture and maybe even changing the colors within that room to create the look of a new space, a space representing a new beginning.

To this day, it is a work in progress for me to hold my tongue in certain rooms within my home when the urge comes over me to hold the position of being right, the battle in which I have chosen to win. However, I was beginning to recognize the difference between having a full-fledged argument full of color, and a light conversational debate, which is healthy.

Ladies and gentlemen, the warmth of your home determines the temperature of your relationship. I know for sure it does. If there has been a time in your life when you've entered a room and feelings of emotion came over you, whether good or bad, then you can understand the feeling I am referring to. So when we open the doors to our home, let the walls speak of memories of laughter and love, and let the crevices exude the warmth of peace, joy, and happiness.

Chapter Two

The Journey of Θ:
Observing Serenity

Serenity is the tranquil balance of heart and mind.

—Harold W. Becker

After a day of studying and working out, my sister-in-law would grab a blank canvas, a smock, paint, paint brushes, palette, rag, a jar of water, and music, all of the things needed for her relaxing project. She'd take all of her painting supplies and set herself up on the front porch. She put on her headphones and began to listen to whatever calms her while she begins to stroke beautiful colors onto the canvas with her fingers and paint brushes. She'd be out on the front porch for hours in her peace. I'd look out the window or walk to the screen door to see what kept her attention. Upon completing painting her masterpiece, she was filled with ideas to share with me regarding writing my books and expanding S.H.E. Publishing, LLC. She was so innovative to the point where she began creating original book covers that would touch the hearts of any author and all readers. Her serenity was the reset button she pushed that gave her a boost of energy and mental health moments, and it rebuilt her emotional bank account, which we will get into later.

That simple act and view of my sister-in-law changed my mindset. I learned from her that I needed to identify my serenity, and I needed to incorporate serenity into my daily tasks. Once I identified my serenity, it helped me to remain calm when things around me were in disarray, it kept me focused on my tranquility, it molded my temperament, and it became contagious.

Serenity for me is the sun shining through the clouds after rain, representing a fresh start. Serenity is waking up to the sound of birds chirping on a summer's day, amplifying joy and new mercy in the morning. Serenity is the time I spend alone that is dedicated to my time spent in the word of God, keeping me humble. Serenity is me waking up to palm trees and the sun sparkling off the water, giving off the reflection of diamonds. Serenity is a lake view adorned with lavender, fuchsia, and yellow flowers surrounded by greenery. Serenity, for me, is what it means to have heaven on earth.

Within the next two moments, I will share how I found serenity in my daily task and how I began to create moments of stillness for my family. These would be moments of exposure to my family's experiences that would build a stronger bond between us, which would also *keep him coming home with love.*

Moment Three:
Identifying Tranquility Daily

Don't wait for the perfect moment, take the moment

and make it perfect.

—Quotesgram.com

One of my dreams came true when I was presented with the opportunity to work in an industry I'd always wanted to partake in—working within the federal judiciary. On good days, my travel time includes a twenty-five- to thirty-minute drive to the Metra train station, a twenty-minute ride on the train, and a ten-minute walk from the train to my place of employment. If I look up into the sky to appreciate my surroundings, that adds five minutes or so to my walk.

There is a street intersection on my way to work where the traffic light turns green on all four corners for pedestrians, giving them the right of way to cross the street vertically, horizontally, or diagonally. I look forward to being able to cross the street diagonally. *That is so cool to me!* To top it off, there is a convenience store kitty-corner from my place of employment, and I sometimes see people who are less fortunate standing around. Still, I know they were standing around for the same reason I walked past the store every morning—in the middle of chaos in the busy city of Chi-Town was the sound of classical music playing. Oh, my soul, this is genius. *In the middle of the chaos is the sound of serenity.*

The convenience store owner played classical music every morning as the people of this world walked by. This was a blessing of peace every morning. And as I walked by, I would ask God each day to bless me with a beautiful day and give me the wisdom to overcome the many work challenges, and He did every time.

I took the moments of my daily travels back and forth to work and made them perfect. But I couldn't stop there. I had to ensure there were those moments of serenity within my home. So on the weekends, I made sure to transfer the positive energy that I'd found within my serenity to my husband and children if I had not done a great job of executing that during the workweek. I wake up early in the morning to make time to create an unobstructed view of the sun shining above the lake in our backyard by opening the sheer silk drapes. I reposition the furniture if it is out of place, moving the chairs neatly under the kitchen table, and I tidy up a bit, removing apparel and shoes left in the common areas, taking them where they belong. I even create the smell of tranquility by spraying a neutral refreshing mist or by starting breakfast. I've heard that the best part of waking up is Folgers coffee in your cup.

If you have not already done so, I challenge you to find serenity in your daily life tasks, whether that means you relax in a warm bubble bath with candles lit, go on staycations or business trips around the world, or simply hang up pictures that create a peaceful view. Finding your serenity can happen at any time, any place, and you must locate that place within your home.

Moment Four:

Sleeping Under the Stars

――――――― ❦ ―――――――

Challenges are what make life interesting; Overcoming them

is what makes life meaningful.

―Joshua J. Marine

My immediate family was invited to go on a camping trip on the hottest weekend of the summer. There were four families on my block, including us, who would be embarking on this neighborhood adventure, which I would later find to be a challenge.

The kids could barely go to sleep the night before our camping trip due to their excitement. They were looking forward to the road trip, and I loved exposing my husband and children to different experiences like this. We packed the entire house because we wanted to make sure we had all we needed, especially since we would be sleeping out in the wilderness.

On the morning of the camping trip, we were ready to roll. The rental car was packed with our gear, supplies, food, and us, *the Burton Billionaires*. The only things we would leave behind is the chaos of electronics and the internet, so I thought.

After four hours of driving, singing songs, playing games, and cracking jokes, we had finally arrived at our destination. We picked up the rules to the camping grounds at the office near the entrance of the camping site. We were informed that there were people who lived near the camping location, and that we needed to respect their domain, because this was their home.

Although we were ready to begin the festivities upon arrival, we spent the entire first day building our one-room suite, blowing up our air mattresses and hanging our lanterns and bug repellant. We thought we had it all until the people two spots from us pulled out a giant projection screen. It was lights, camera, and action. Come to find out, we were surrounded by several families who were related, and every year they would go camping together. At that moment, I was happy to be surrounded by the love of these families. This made me feel a sense of belonging and it made me feel that we were all in this together.

The kids played games, made up things to do, colored, played with water, had scavenger hunts, and talked with each other. They were beginning to build a closer bond with the children in the neighborhood, the children they'd see on the school bus, to and from school, but never really chatted with. My daughters were learning the value of teamwork and friendships on a different level. There was also time allotted for the married couples to build a bond and actually pay attention to each other without the distraction of everyday responsibility.

In the hot sun, amid the beauty of nature, surrounded by enormous trees, there was no wearing makeup or lashes, or looking cute in high heels. I had to exude that natural beauty. Well, at least that is what I had hoped to do. Overall, we were having lots of healthy fun without any electronics. We were away from the chaos of the world at that moment.

As the day moved into the afternoon and the afternoon moved into night, we ended our evening with several families seated in front of that big screen. Movie night was fantastic, not to mention we were greeted with a delicious spread prepared by the heads of the households—*the men*. You would think this would be the ending of a successful evening, but what would come next would take the cake.

After an excellent movie in the wilderness, it was time to shower and get comfortable sleeping in our one-room suite called a tent. We walked to the bathrooms, which resembled the bathrooms in an elementary school. The only difference was they were outside and not inside a building. Walking into the stalls, we were greeted with a smell of nature—and not the right kind of nature. The water in the toilet stalls and the sink faucets were a reddish-pink and smelled like the sewers. The water was contaminated. No wonder I was told to bring several jugs of water when going camping. We would be brushing our teeth and washing our hands and faces for the duration of this trip with bottled water. This is the moment I became grateful to have bottled water and even more thankful that we have regulations prohibiting the contamination of water in residential areas.

Walking into the shower with my two youngest daughters unveiled a disgusting sight. The showers had doors like the bathroom stalls, the walls and floors were a filthy, deep brown and khaki color, and the water that came down from the showerhead was a dull, clear brown. *What happened to the crystal-clear water?* If you didn't keep your mouth closed tight, little particles of water would splash inside. Can you imagine having to bring two babies into a filthy-looking shower?

One of my daughters began to take off her water shoes, and I screamed as if she had done something horrible. That was it. I had to get out of there. I was not clean, my babies were not clean, but at this point, I didn't care. As far as I was concerned, I did not want to drink or eat anything the next day.

I could not bear going into those bathrooms or shower stalls the next day. Although that hideous sight made me have nightmares that night, we still ended the night in silence under a bed of stars in our one-bedroom loft. Amid the silence, we would be interrupted by my oldest daughter asking, "When are we going home?"

The next morning, my children and husband awoke to the Housewives of Rolling Meadows (which is how we referred to ourselves) cooking in the hot kitchen of nature. Again, it was the hottest weekend of summer, and the little sprinkles of water that touched my skin the prior evening from that dreadful shower experience certainly did not help with what I would smell like if I didn't get to a body of clean water quickly.

After breakfast, I took another quick look at the map and realized there was a solution to our no-shower problem. Day two would be the day we would all venture to the on-site water park and the huge bathtub, otherwise known as the pool. As we approached the pool, I could envision us all running in slow motion to the song "Run to You" by Whitney Houston. We were finally able to bathe in water that looked clear and pure blue. The women and children were at the water park and pool the entire day, while the men went hunting for food and enjoyed the peace of fishing.

After our fun, adventurous, and clean day at the water park, we headed back to the camping site, because it was nearing lunch. Someone needed something from the store, and I immediately jumped up and said I would get whatever we needed. I even offered to pay for it. This would be my chance to go to the bathroom at the nearby Walmart. All I can tell you is that I had never been so happy to be in the bathroom of a Walmart. I must have stayed in that bathroom for fifteen minutes. As strange as it sounds, I was in heaven, and that is when I knew the meaning of being blessed and the importance of appreciating the little things in life.

Upon Jermaine and I arriving back at the camping site, I had made up my mind that my family was going home on this day. I would not win the hardship of this camping challenge. I could not deal with it anymore. With that said, I knew that we had all learned the value of being together and appreciating what we had and where we lived. I could have stuck it out, but at that moment, I was mentally conquered by this challenge.

In this life, we have been given the ability to choose. We have the choice to move on, or we have the option to stay in certain circumstances, even if they are not suitable for us. My husband, children, and I certainly have a greater appreciation for our life from our first camping experience. And that experience made us appreciate each other much more.

Thinking back to the moments during the camping trip, I wish I would have taken full advantage of that experience because the little that we did endure made such an impact on my family. I missed out on that opportunity, but that's the beauty of life and a new day: it's not too late to try it again.

Chapter three

The Journey of V:

Valuing Relationships

I think that when the dust settles, we will realize how very

little we need, how very much we have, and the true value of

human connection.

—Thinking Humanity

H ave life experiences made you realize the value of relationships? Have you ever experienced a tragic moment, and the presence of a close friend made it easier for you to cope? As a matter of fact, are you doing your part and bringing value to your relationships by helping make the good times greater and the hard times easier?

Learning to value relationships began with me looking into my mother's eyes as a child and feeling the warmth of her unconditional love. She taught me that people come into your life for a reason, a season, and maybe even a lifetime. And although she shows me the importance of building valuable relationships and friendships, this didn't happen until high school for me.

Attending Marie Sklowdowska Curie Metropolitan High School is when I met three of my closest friends: Sharaka, Latoya, and Rayya. The beauty of our relationship was that we were different in so many ways, which gave us the opportunity to grow from each other. It left no room for competition, envy, or jealousy. I admired and appreciated the differences between the four of us.

I loved my three best friends, and if I were in communication with all of them in this present day, I would communicate to them how much they mean to me. In my heart, these three friends are the sisters I never had. Of the four of us, I was the one who started a family first, and that dream for me came true in my early twenties.

My journey of getting married, having children, and starting my career became my everything, and I began to drop the ball on my friendship responsibilities. While I went hard for my family, I had not considered that I was abandoning my friendships and extended family. I had the hustle mentality of an only child, unlike my mother, who had seven siblings.

Being the only child was me having the mindset of not trusting anyone, and aside from my parents, I had the responsibility of making it in this world alone. This mentality lead me to the abandonment I made my husband feel. In my eyes, my life's order was God first, family and friends second, and career third. However, my actions did not reflect this belief. In practice, I was putting my career first, God second, and family and friends last. I was not building strong foundational relationships. This is difficult to admit, especially knowing that, through all of this, God has always put me first, carried me when I could not walk any further, and continued to fill my cup as it overflowed with blessings upon blessings. Words cannot express how grateful I am, and therefore I honor Him in all that I do.

Looking into the mirror and being brutally honest with oneself is what is needed to move forward. I used to think everyone worked as hard as I worked and that they would not notice my lack of effort in our friendship, because they would be doing the same thing: working hard on what their heart desired. I didn't realize their hearts still desired valuing friendships, which added a balance to their lives. I had to go back to those moments in my life and remember my mother's teachings, and I had to look in the mirror and take ownership of what failed in those relationships, including the relationship with my man.

Having true friendship is an experience I had never known, nor was I interested in learning it at that time in my life. What I didn't realize was that I'd be inspired by the bond my husband had created with his friends, and it wasn't until then that I realized I longed for those same types of friendships. I also didn't realize that by making that balance in my life, it would be beneficial to me, and it would also *keep him coming home with love.*

Moment Five:
The Company He Keeps

❦

Show me your friends and I'll show you your future.

—Unknown

Watching my husband with his friends over the years served to alter my view of friendships. His friendships were different from those I had ever known. This was when I began to see the true value of friendship, but this is also when I realized that this man, this fine brother, would bring value to my life in many ways that I had not anticipated.

Jermaine and I started our family early in life, which resulted in my husband being the only man in his circle who was married. That famous saying "Birds of a feather flock together" became more relatable as I witnessed him acting like the single friends he had rather than the married family man he was. Growing up, he had a great role model and father figure in his life—the man who swept his mother off her feet and who would later adopt him as his son. However, this example still did not stop my husband from acting like a single man.

As the years went by and his friends began to marry, I started to see a shift in his movements and mindset. He began to act like the husband I needed him to be, and in my eyes, he was becoming a significant role model and mentor for his friends and family.

I wanted us to begin setting the expectation of surrounding ourselves with people and friends with the same goals and values we had, friends who could have different viewpoints and not be judgmental, and friends who did not want my man's attention because of what their own relationships were lacking.

Having married friends and single friends was of value. It is what I call building healthy relationships and finding balance. My single friends brought value to my life, because they helped me not lose myself within my marriage, and my married friends brought value to my life by sharing their experiences, experiences that I could relate to, which kept me clearheaded.

I've come to realize that just because you are hanging out with other married couples does not mean you necessarily share the same standards and values, and by the same token, just because you have a single friend doesn't mean they will be a bad influence on you. We can learn and grow from both sets of friends. However, we must remember and value the role we currently hold as husband and wife.

When just about all of my husband's friends were

married, I saw them trying to be better men, praying for each other, sharing knowledge and insight, working hard, and inspiring each other. Jermaine and his close friends communicated virtually every day. Before COVID-19, they'd go on guys trips every year, and they'd regularly celebrate each other's accomplishments.

It took years and years for me to finally realize I needed and wanted that type of bond with my friends. I was an only child, and before this, I had never yearned for those type of relationships. Deep down inside, I think I just didn't want to feel the hurt if those relationships did not succeed. You see, I had my husband, my four daughters, my father, and my mother. My mother is my ace, and she always has my best interest at heart, and she will always be by my side. But what happens when my mother or father are not near, or if Jermaine goes through a midlife crisis and we go our separate ways? How would I cope with life's challenges when they're not around and I don't have real authentic friendships to help me through those challenging moments?

I realized I had to recreate that balance in my life. It was time for me to rebuild my relationship with at least one of my best friends and begin building intentional friendships with others who had become an inspiration to my life. I've learned that *"Good friends are like stars. You don't always see them, but you know they're always there!"* (source unknown). I also needed to prioritize my life in the correct order, truly putting my God first, family and friends second, and career third.

Moment Six:
My Man Is My Rock;
My Child Is My Gem

❧

In my husband I know true love.

In my children I know pure love.

—PicLab

Valuing relationships is about investing in and inspiring ourselves, our family, and our friends. Starting a publishing company has not only led me to want to invest, inspire, and learn by reading more, but it also prompted an idea for Father's Day that would express a meaningful message to my husband and my daughters simultaneously.

A week before Father's Day, the girls and I were in Target with a strategy to get only what was on our list of needs, but as usual when we go into Target, I spend no less than one hundred ($100.00) dollars; *it happens every time. Can you relate?* The marketers for Target sure know how to pull me in with the vibrant colors and friendly service. It's to the point where I find myself purchasing items just because of the feel and sleekness of the setup.

As my daughters and I came upon the book section, I began imagining that one day my books would be sitting on the shelves within the book section of Target stores and globally around the world. *That would be a dream come true for me.* I even thought about placing my book on an empty bookshelf just so I could see it there. I just could not stop envisioning this.

In my newfound world of writing, reading, and publishing, I have begun to appreciate the value of books from a new perspective. As I stood staring at the bookshelves in Target, there it was! It sat in the children's section on the third row from the bottom, peeking out at me with soft, calming colors. On the front cover of this book there was an illustration of a father and his daughter. It could have been a father and his stepdaughter. It was called *Hair Love*, by Matthew A. Cherry, illustrated by Vashti Harrison. I remembered first seeing these illustrated characters on YouTube, and as I watched the story, it brought tears to my eyes. It was a very touching story. It's a must-see if you have not seen it on YouTube, or go to your local stores to pick up the book.

I grabbed a copy of *Hair Love* along with three other daddy-daughter books. I made my way to the register, paid the bill, and the girls and I headed home. As we pulled into the driveway, my emotions were full of excitement! I couldn't wait to go into the house and custom package the books with S.H.E. Publishing, LLC's gift wrap.

Father's Day had arrived, and I could not wait for Jermaine to wake up so we could sing to him and spend the entire day with him. He and I make it a point to spend holidays and birthdays together, which I fully elaborate on in part I of *Keep Him Coming Home with Love: Be Intentional about Strengthening Your Bond.* The day began with my two youngest daughters jumping all over him to awake him on his special day. This would be the Father's Day where my gifts would not be expensive, but they'd be worth gold.

After breakfast and more fun, we began to present Jermaine with several Father's Day cards, which expressed precisely the words we wanted to convey. It's amazing how the creative authors of Hallmark cards seem to know exactly how you feel inside. This shows me that we're all connected, and we're all characters within our own story going through the same types of situations within the different moments of our lives.

It was time for Jermaine to open his gift of gold. Our youngest baby girl walked toward him and presented him with his beautifully wrapped gift. As he began to unwrap, he put the books on the table one by one as he read each title: *I Love Dad with The Very Hungry Caterpillar* by Eric Carle; *Dad by*

My Side by Soosh; *I Love Daddy Every Day* by Isabel Otter; and *Hair Love* by Matthew A. Cherry. He then looked at me and said, "Thanks, but where is the real gift?" Okay, so this was supposed to be a sentimental moment, and at that very moment, we all just chuckled because he wouldn't be Jermaine if he didn't say something amusing. But that evening, and every evening since, he reads every book received on his special day to Jordyn and Jade, our two youngest daughters.

Shenitha Finesse Anniece Burton

Chapter Four

The Journey of Æ:
Evening Tones with a Splash of Color

Fashion is art and you are the canvas.

—Velvet Paper

H ave you found the uniqueness of who you are? As a matter of fact, have you been intentional about bringing that uniqueness and splash of color to the presence of your relationships?

I've known my husband for over twenty-five years, and to keep the attention of someone for so long, I had to realize my splash of color and continue to bring that splash of color to our relationship.

Throughout my marriage, there were times when I had to find myself and keep finding myself. And you ask, "Why is this?" Because when you're married, you want to be all that you can be for your husband, and you want to show him that you are deserving of him. But then you begin to get comfortable and forget all the reasons he became attracted to you, and you can lose yourself. You stop doing what grabbed his attention when you first met, and that is merely you being who you are.

Within the next two moments, I will give you a visual of how I intentionally brought that splash of color to our relationship by having fun and creating fantasies, but first, I will explain how I had to maintain emotional stability by keeping an eighty-twenty mindset, which would keep me sane, and *keep him coming home with love.*

Moment Seven:
Keep A Positive Balance in Your Emotional Bank Account

What we see depends mainly on what we look for.

—John Lubbock

The year 2020 has been by far a year to remember. In reflecting, there have been moments of hope, but there have also been unforgettable and heartbreaking moments that include: the death of the Kobe "Mamba" Bryant, his daughter, and several passengers in a helicopter crash; the COVID-19 pandemic that affected the love language of touch; the death of George Floyd, Brionna Taylor, and others that caused riots and peaceful protesting; the death of our Black Panther and superhero Chadwick Boseman; and the uncertainty of our world's new normal. With all of this negativity, if I had not been in the practice of keeping my emotional bank account at a positive balance, I could easily become emotionally stagnant and depressed. But because my mentality is to look at the glass half full, I recognized that the year 2020 would also give us an opportunity to reflect on what really matters, spend more time with family, and realize the importance of mental health.

One morning as I sat in the private room of my doctor's office waiting to receive my annual checkup, I began gazing out of the window. The sunlight pierced through the shades, creating a striped pattern on the wall. Although I was viewing serenity in that moment, my daily duties for the day occupied my thoughts: *What bills will I pay? What's on the menu for dinner? Will it be yo-yo (you're on your own) time for the family?*

When the doctor walked into the room where I sat comfortably, she informed me that she felt a lump on my breast. She gave me the order and paperwork to see a specialist. My mindset and emotional state changed from positive thinking and living life to worry, fear, stress, and sickness all at once. This was a moment in my life that I've only shared with my mother and husband until now. I felt sick to my stomach sitting in that doctor's office. It was all the "what ifs" I was thinking about that got me to the point where I could not function. So after all the serenity, and after all of the moments of peace in the word of God, I cracked. When we face unwelcome news, tragedies, deaths, and other horrible situations, why does the mind go straight to negativity, sadness, and a feeling of doom? Why does the mindset suddenly shift when we've experienced plenty of moments of good?

Fast-forward to my appointment with the specialist. I received fantastic news that there was no sign of cancer, thank goodness. Before knowing the results, I'd gone through weeks and weeks of hidden stress and depression, all to hear that good news. After that moment, it became my goal to truly learn how to build a stable, healthy, and bulletproof mindset.

I knew I had to have positive places of peace in my home and at my workplace. I knew I had to have supportive family, friends, mentors, and coaches. I knew I had to finally make my vision of having an eighty-twenty mindset a reality. Most importantly, I needed a man I did not have to persuade to keep coming home but a man who wanted to come home.

My vision of having an eighty-twenty mindset starts with the seeds of wisdom that God has placed in me. I have listened, and I have been observant of the thoughtful inspiration placed in my mind and the imagery placed before my eyes, one being the moment I walked into the office of my strengths coach Beverly Griffeth-Bryant. I saw an inspirational quote on her wall, and it read, "Speak what you seek until you see what you've said." Let me say that again. "Speak what you seek until you see what you've said." And ever since that day, that is what I have done. *S.H.E.*

Publishing, LLC will be the Apple of book publishing, and it will be the buffet for all authors. My family will live an abundant life, and we are the Burton Billionaires. I am speaking what I seek until I see what I've said, and I charge you to speak what you seek until you see what you've said.

So let's get back to when I sat in the doctor's office and faced the challenging moment of thinking I had breast cancer. In my mind, I began to speak the negative version of what was to come; *that represents the 20 percent.* I had to be realistic about the possibility that I may have had breast cancer. However, I should have also been speaking positive outcomes; *that represents the 80 percent.*

There would be a day when my faith and mindset would be tested again. The day the sound of silence became a constant buzzing in my ear is the day I lost the hearing in my left ear. I was diagnosed with pneumonia, and it was coupled with harmful bacteria that lead to the unfriendly outcome of me losing the hearing in my left ear. When I'd shut the TV off and the house was completely silent, I could hear a buzzing noise in my left ear. Today, that buzzing continues to be a constant irritation, which has now become my silence, and guess what, I am okay with it, because it could be worse.

I was prepared for this new challenge that I had to embark on. Listening to Joel Osteen, Pastor Jacob A. Pickett Jr. of

New Smyrna Church of God and Christ in Gary, Indiana, the pastors of First Baptist Church in Hammond, Indiana, and the friendships I'd finally built helped me through this. I also listened to other inspirational messages and affirmations via YouTube. Those lessons and sermons would prepare me to have a balanced perception and see the good in life, and they would help me to be strong in the challenging moments that would inevitably come my way.

I have been told that therapy is revitalizing and serves as a great retreat, and the decision to seek counseling has been one of the best experiences and decisions some people have confessed to having. At this moment in time, my form of counseling is writing my story and being transparent in what I share.

In closing, with every challenge, I found myself dropping to my knees throughout each day and praying for my family, friends, neighbors, and coworkers. My husband would catch me on my knees every so often but didn't think anything of it. He probably thought I had a stomachache due to the chips I'd snuck into bed, or the cheese danish and ice cream I had eaten before going to bed the prior evening. Jermaine never knew that I would say a little prayer for us and our family every day as I woke because I believed in prayer.

Moment Eight:
Fantasy Island

If one is lucky, a solitary fantasy can totally

transform one million realities.

—Maya Angelou

After ensuring my emotions were in the right place, it was time to make some intentional fun. I'd wake up early in the morning on the weekends, and after tidying up, I'd do the following: (1) put on my workout outfit; (2) pull my hair back into a sleek ponytail; (3) splash some water on my hair and face; (4) pop in a workout tape or pull up a YouTube work twerk video in the basement; (5) lay out my mat; (6) grab a water bottle and weights; and (7) do all of this with a garbage bag wrapped around my stomach. As Jermaine woke up and came where I was in his man cave, he sees the sweat on my face made from the sprinkles of water, and he realizes I am trying to keep that body just right for him. That kicked on a switch in his head, and he was instantly intrigued. He may not have shown it immediately, but I knew I succeeded in my intentional scheme when I was later greeted with a smile and an invitation to one of our places of peace.

There are several fantasies I have created to keep that splash of color, spice, and fun in my relationship with my significant other. I call them fantasy challenges. Another fantasy challenge that continues to work in my relationship is the cooking challenge. It involves purchasing a delicious meal, putting it in the oven, frying onions and green peppers on the stovetop to give the house that perfect aroma, putting on my apron, splashing myself with flour, and looking low-key cute. Dinner is then served on a platter in more than one way.

After executing a few fantasies based on what I know my husband likes, these fantasies began to transform into positive realities. I wanted to start working out and cooking delicious meals more often than not. These created fantasies are an example of faking it until you make it, or as I say, "acting my way up." Now, perhaps you have it all put together, and you don't have to create these intimate moments called fantasies, but it's really all about keeping the fun, excitement, and fire in your relationship.

I charge you with coming up with and executing a fantasy for your mate, or maybe try the workout fantasy, and see how your spouse reacts. To be effective, it must be something your significant other is interested in. Afterward, capture the memory of his response in a journal entry to yourself, because it will be worth keeping and remembering as you *keep him coming home with love*.

Parting Thoughts

Until we meet again, *keep him coming home with love* by valuing the real estate of your home and your marriage, and know that the warmth of your home determines the temperature of your relationship. The goal is to create your playbook for a successful marriage because the struggle of retaining and maintaining a triumphant marriage is real, but it's a beautiful journey. Also, keep these learning points in mind:

Moment One: What I learned from this moment, "The Entrance to the Kingdom," is that it is essential that the feel of your home is warm and welcoming. This experience can include a pleasant aroma, soothing colors on the walls, and the strategic arrangement of your living spaces.

Remember that the beauty of relationships and living life is that it's never to later to begin again and press that restart button. When married, you have the obligation and ability to create those needed moments of restart, and it doesn't always have to be at a milestone moment or year within your relationship. This, my friend, will continue to *keep him coming home with love.*

Moment Two: What I learned from this moment, "Rooms of Passion and Peace," is that it is vital to value the real estate of your home and your marriage. The rooms within your home should be sacred and be associated with peace and tranquility. Designating rooms in your home for meetings, study time, arguments, and fun, and being mindful of the company you keep can contribute to the success of your journey with your significant other, and it *will keep him coming home with love.*

Moment Three: What I learned from this moment, "Identifying Tranquility Daily," is that we should open our eyes to the beauty of the environment we have right before our eyes. We can create those picture-perfect moments for ourselves by valuing the landscape of what we see, the architecture of the buildings that surround us, and the inside of the homes that we live in. Identify your serenity, because it will keep you at peace, and you will have the strength to *keep him coming home with love.*

Moment Four: What I learned from this moment, "Sleeping Under the Stars," is that spending time away from the chaos of electronics is an opportunity to build stronger bonds with the people you value in your life. Viewing the beauty of nature can be calming and humbling. It's an amazing source of creativity and purity. Viewing nature can also contribute to you finding and keeping yourself and being thankful for those who you have, and it will certainly *keep him coming home with love.*

Moment Five: What I learned from this moment, "The Company He Keeps," is that there is value in building and maintaining friendships. It's a necessity. I learned from my husband the true meaning of friendship and how you must surround yourself with genuine people who love you, and that you must also contribute by doing your part and being an honest friend and extended family member. Add to the value of others, and this will contribute to your relations and *keep him coming home with love.*

Moment Six: What I learned from this moment, "My Man is my Rock; My Child is my Gem," is that my husband must feel that we are one, and I must ensure my children know that I love them unconditionally, and that I am forever their advocate and lifelong supporter. The love for my husband and the love for my daughters is a different type of love. Our men are our Captain Americas, and our children, whether in a blended family or not, must remain our gems and diamonds in the rough until our guidance sharpens them. The quality of our relationships with our spouse and our children is paramount, and it will not only *keep him coming home with love*, but it will *keep our children coming home with love* every time.

Moment Seven: What I learned from this moment, "Keep A Positive Balance in Your Emotional Account," is that it's essential to lead with positivity in situations when we are faced with challenging situations. I have also learned that by displaying this mindset and mentality, others will see how you deal with your struggles, and that will make a profound impact on their lives.

Identifying the people, places, and things that generate a deposit or withdrawal in and out of your emotional bank account is key to keeping a positive balance. "Knowing your worth, honoring your worth, and sharing your worth maintains that balanced emotional account." The JAS Team (*Joan K. Moore, Anniece Anderson-Owens, and Shenitha Finesse Anniece Burton)* are three woman who deliver presentations to men and women about this subject matter, and it will equip you with the tools you need to *keep him coming home with love*.

Moment Eight: What I learned from this moment, "Fantasy Island," is that there is something motivating and inspiring about creating fun fantasies within your relationship. Each and every one of us is unique in our own way. Find what that is that makes you unique, and shine bright like the diamond that you are.

It is important not to compromise your integrity and lose yourself creating fun fantasies, although they have the potential of becoming a reality. Your confidence must not remove the humbleness in all that you do. I don't pretend to be an expert at how men think, but I know a man can appreciate a fun, confident, and humble woman with integrity.

The mind is very powerful, and we can be the innovators of our relationships by being the best at who we are, bringing our splash of color, and being purposeful in our doings, and this will *keep him coming home with love.*

Keep Him Coming Home with Love

Acknowledgments

I would like to thank my Father, God, husband, Jermaine, and daughters Jada, Jasmyn, Jordyn, and Jade for being the inspiration for me writing this book series. If it had not been for your love, the memories we created, and the experiences we've shared, I would not have been able to write this book. I love you more than you know, and I will continue to protect you the best way that I can while I am here with you. And when we are apart, I will pray that you continue to come home with love.

I would also like to thank my team, who helped support and encourage my writing and publishing a book full of valuable content. My professional team includes my brother and sister from another mother, Ankur Patel and Zarna Patel, S.H.E. Publishing, LLC's Team (She-Squad), J-Camille Productions, SB Décor, and Elite Authors.

I want to thank the people and entities who had no idea I was writing this book. Still, they were inspiring me along the way unknowingly: the New Smyrna Church of God in Christ lead by Pastor Jacob A. Pickett Jr. and First Lady Belinda Pickett;

my dad, Robert Hoskins, who played basketball in a church while I wrote on a chalkboard in another room of the sanctuary; my step-father, Kenneth Owens; my in-laws, Mr. and Mrs. Christopher Burton; Ms. Diane Shula and Mr. Niznik (former teachers at Overton Elementary School); CEO of Leader by Design, Joan K. Moore; my strengths coach, Beverly Griffeth-Bryant; the owner and family of Cummins Remodeling, Mr. and Mrs. Russ Cummins; Mr. and Mrs. Mondale Jamison; and the women and men who participated in the special project of *Keep Him Coming Home with Love: The Architecture of a Resilient Woman*. I love them all and wish them continued success in their marriages.

And to my ace, I could not live life without you. My lovely mother helped me throughout this process, and she has been present during every moment revealed in this book. Because of her shared experiences, I have been able to be dependable, hold myself accountable, and lead with strength and confidence from any seat that I've held. My mother has always been my biggest supporter and advocate. My mother is my motivation, and she continues to inspire me every day of my life. Mama, I love you, later.

Also By

Shenitha Finesse Anniece Burton

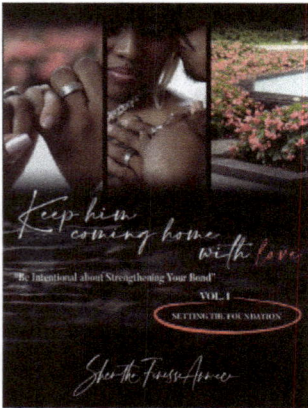

Keep Him Coming Home with Love: Be Intentional about Strengthening Your Bond

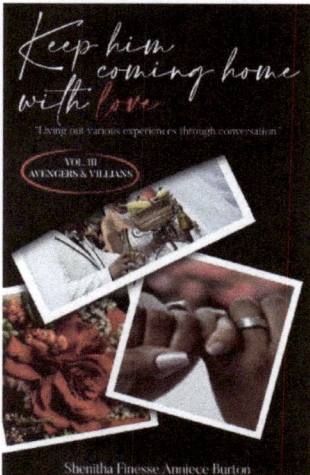

Coming Soon!

Keep Him Coming Home with Love: Living Out Various Experiences through Conversation

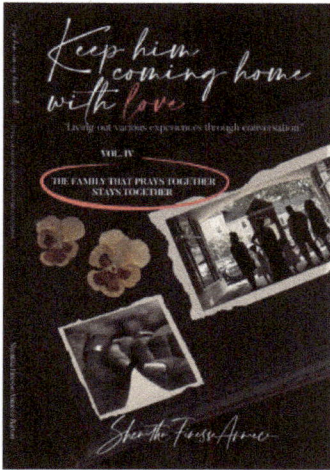

Keep Him Coming Home with Love:

The Family That Prays Together

Stays Together

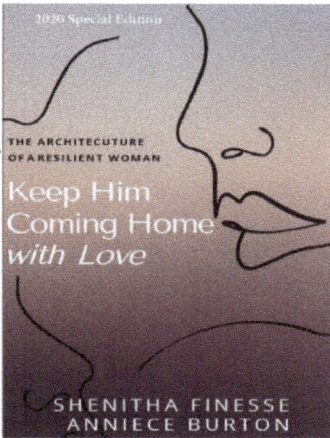

Keep Him Coming Home with Love:

The Architecture of a Resilient

Woman

About the Author

Born to parents Anniece Anderson-Owens and Robert Hoskins, Shenitha Finesse Anniece Burton grew up in Chicago, Illinois, in the Robert Taylor projects, where she lived in the same home with her mom, aunties, uncles, and cousins. She attended Overton Elementary School, Marie Sklowdowska Curie High School, Pivot Point Hair School, Northwestern Business College majoring in paralegal studies; Purdue Calumet University majoring in sociology with a criminal justice option, and Michigan State University in its nonbearing certificate program.

In Burton's lifetime, she has been employed at McDonald's as a cashier and fry cook, at Ford City Movie Theater as the concession stand servant, at UPS as a loader, and with the federal courts, where she worked hard and was committed to delivering high-quality work, professional leadership, and creative solutions. Burton settled down professionally when she was employed with the US courts, where she was promoted through the ranks. Starting from the lowest rung of the ladder gave her an appreciation of hard work and dedication. She remains humble in all that she does, and she tries hard to put others before herself. Burton realizes that growing her leadership abilities and becoming aware of her signature themes have helped her to find passion in everything she does. She is a strengths champion who leads with developer, learner, input, futuristic, relator, achiever, self-assurance, responsibility, includer, and analytical capabilities.

Burton's hobbies consist of eating dessert before dinner, public speaking, writing nonfiction books, skating, playing the piano, reading, hanging out in the driveway or the backyard with neighbors, and vacationing with her family. Burton is a lifelong learner.